CELEBRATING THE NAME SHARON

Celebrating the Name Sharon

Walter the Educator

Silent King Books

Copyright © 2024 by Walter the Educator

All rights reserved. No part of this book may be reproduced in any manner whatsoever without written permission except in the case of brief quotations embodied in critical articles and reviews.

First Printing, 2024

Disclaimer
This book is a literary work; poems are not about specific persons, locations, situations, and/or circumstances unless mentioned in a historical context. This book is for entertainment and informational purposes only. The author and publisher offer this information without warranties expressed or implied. No matter the grounds, neither the author nor the publisher will be accountable for any losses, injuries, or other damages caused by the reader's use of this book. The use of this book acknowledges an understanding and acceptance of this disclaimer.

dedicated to everyone with the first name of Sharon

SHARON

In valleys deep, where echoes sleep,

SHARON

Resides a name, Sharon, pure and sweet,

SHARON

Upon the lips, a melody, a treat,

SHARON

In whispers soft, its secrets keep.

SHARON

Sharon, a beacon in the night,

SHARON

Guiding ships with gentle light,

SHARON

Through storms that rage with all their might,

SHARON

Her name, a harbor, safe and right.

SHARON

In fields adorned with blooms so fair,

SHARON

Sharon dances without a care,

SHARON

Her laughter fills the fragrant air,

SHARON

A symphony beyond compare.

SHARON

Through forests dense with ancient trees,

SHARON

Sharon wanders, her spirit free,

SHARON

Each step a tale, each breath a plea,

SHARON

For beauty in simplicity.

SHARON

In dreams, she roams on wings of gold,

SHARON

In realms where wonders yet unfold,

SHARON

Her name, a story yet untold,

SHARON

In every star that's bright and bold.

SHARON

Sharon, a name that holds the key,

SHARON

To realms of possibility,

SHARON

In every heart, a reverie,

SHARON

Of hope and love eternally.

SHARON

So let us raise our voices high,

SHARON

And sing the praises of Sharon's sky,

SHARON

Where dreams take flight and never die,

SHARON

In every tear and every sigh.

SHARON

For Sharon, dear Sharon, hear our song,

SHARON

In every note, where we belong,

SHARON

A symphony that shall prolong,

SHARON

The legacy of Sharon, strong.

SHARON

In every echo, in every rhyme,

SHARON

Sharon's name shall stand the test of time,

SHARON

A beacon in the dark, a sign,

SHARON

Of love and light that's ever mine.

SHARON

And when the stars in heaven gleam,

SHARON

And moonlight casts its silver beam,

SHARON

Sharon's name, a radiant beam,

SHARON

In every heart, a cherished dream.

SHARON

ABOUT THE CREATOR

Walter the Educator is one of the pseudonyms for Walter Anderson. Formally educated in Chemistry, Business, and Education, he is an educator, an author, a diverse entrepreneur, and he is the son of a disabled war veteran. "Walter the Educator" shares his time between educating and creating. He holds interests and owns several creative projects that entertain, enlighten, enhance, and educate, hoping to inspire and motivate you.

Follow, find new works, and stay up to date
with Walter the Educator™
at WaltertheEducator.com

www.ingramcontent.com/pod-product-compliance
Lightning Source LLC
LaVergne TN
LVHW052010060526
838201LV00059B/3942